1·14·72

BILLY GRAHAM

TALKS WITH

DAVID FROST

BILLY GRAHAM

TALKS WITH

DAVID FROST

BY DAVID FROST

A. J. HOLMAN COMPANY

division of J. B. Lippincott Company

Philadelphia and New York

U.S. Library of Congress Cataloging in Publication Data

Frost, David.
  Billy Graham talks with David Frost.

  1. Graham, William Franklin, birth date
I. Graham, William Franklin, birth date   II. Title.
BV3785. G69F76   201   77-39674
ISBN-0-87981-005-X

Photographic credits

Billy Graham Evangelistic Association: Pages 15, 18, 37, 42, 45, 47, 67, 88
Group W Productions: Pages 2, 6, 13, 51, 92
Religious News Service Photo: Pages 21, 24, 34, 53, 56, 64, 68, 71, 74, 81
Wide World Photo: Page 32

1653134

Contents

Foreword

It's a great joy to introduce this little book made up of my two television interviews with Billy Graham.

How well I remember the first time I saw him when he was speaking in London at Harringay Arena. I was only fifteen then.

Later I met him and we have become great friends. I always enjoy talking to Billy Graham—on camera or off.

May you enjoy this account of our conversations.

DAVID FROST

Introduction

THIS IS NOT AN ORDINARY BOOK. In fact, it lacks chapters and organization, but therein lies its charm.

Here you pull up a chair beside two good friends engaged in an ambling, often deeply revealing conversation. You feel close to Billy Graham, the North Carolina dairyman's son who is evangelist and friend to the mighty and the lowly. Prodding him and encouraging him is David Frost, the canny, often dead pan interviewer, who was nurtured in a Methodist parsonage in England and is now acclaimed as a top television personality on two continents.

Have you any ideas about the geography of heaven or hell; Do you think the planets are inhabited? Is Richard Nixon anything like Lyndon Johnson? And, oh yes, do you know why the Grahams serve oyster stew for breakfast on Christmas Day, or why Billy talks German to his dogs.

In a conversation between two good friends like Billy Graham and David Frost, there's a place for incidents or recollections that may, at first glance, seem trivial, yet reveal a man's profoundest qualities. In this unstructured give and take of unrehearsed discussion, one is able to comprehend the greatness, the simplicity, the humanity of a religious leader who is readily understood by the mighty and the lowly.

[9]

There are some very poignant moments. Without bathos, Billy Graham expresses his love for his wife. As exemplar, teaches us how to have a happy marriage and how to get along with people. No wonder presidents, and long-haired youths, and untold throngs are captivated by Billy Graham.

The book is a transcript of two ninety-minute television interviews—one conducted in New York in June, 1969, in the first week of the David Frost Show and one in London just before Christmas in 1970.

BILLY GRAHAM

TALKS WITH

DAVID FROST

Telecast from London

FROST: May I introduce Billy Graham. APPLAUSE. We thought it would be nice to do this program in London and it's so good to be talking again with Billy Graham. Our first ever conversation for television, many years ago now, was right here wasn't it?

GRAHAM: Right here, I think in this studio wasn't it?

FROST: Yes, right here and it's eighteen months since we talked in New York.

GRAHAM: That's right, I think I was on your first show. Was that correct?

FROST: Right, absolutely, the first week of the David Frost Show in New York. And here we are talking in London and talking to people in America from London. Lots has happened in the last eighteen months, Billy, and there are a lot of things I'd like to talk to you about—one happening that mercifully had a happy ending just a week or two ago when there was the attempt on the life of another great spiritual leader, the Pope. I wonder what your feelings were when you read about that?

[13]

GRAHAM: Well, of course, I was shocked like everyone else because I was amazed that anyone could even get that close to the Pope who didn't have proper credentials. Then the second thing, I think, was how quickly bishops can become rather active in violence to protect what they believe in, you see. And I'm just thankful, I'm sure with the rest of the world, that his life was spared.

FROST: It raised the thought for me, knowing we were going to talk, do you have many threats? Have you ever had an attack made on you, or threats made on your life?

GRAHAM: David, yes. We have constant threats, as a matter of fact, five people in one week tried to get to my home. Most of them are mental cases. The police had to deal with two or three of them. Yes, we do have this type of thing, so much so that we had to build a fence around my home and, upon security advice, we got three attack dogs—one living in the house and two outside. They're under complete control, of course. They were trained in Germany and given to me by a friend in Philadelphia. Unfortunately we have reached that stage of violence in some sections of the country. I suppose it's true with people who are rather well-known, and especially religious and political figures who are speaking out on the issues of today. We have a lot of people today who are under the influence of drugs, and we have all sorts of people that are mentally disturbed. Over one half of all the hospital beds in the United States are occupied by mental patients. Only a handful of all mental patients are confined; most mental patients are still on the outside. And they are after people like you and me, so you've got to be careful when you come back to the U.S.

Ruth Graham, Billy's wife, is the charming hostess of the Graham homey, country-style mountain home. She is shown here with her constant companion, a highly trained Doberman Pinscher.

FROST: I'm still terrified about those three dogs of yours. Do they understand English as well as German?

GRAHAM: No, they don't. We have to speak to them in German.

FROST: Really?

GRAHAM: Yes.

FROST: You really do?

GRAHAM: We have sixteen commands that we give them in German, and if you came to visit us, they'd be very nice. In fact, one of them would probably lick you to death in welcoming you. But they can change in an instant upon command, and they become vicious, snarling animals. We've never had to use them, thank the Lord. I don't think I could ever give a command, no matter what was happening, for one of them to attack someone. But I think just their being there is sort of a deterrent, because they are big and they are pretty vicious looking. The one that lives indoors is a big Dobermann Pinscher, highly-trained and very powerful, with 1,500 pounds of bite in his jaws, which could sever a man's arm. But he's very sweet and very nice and welcomes everybody. LAUGHTER — The only thing that would change him would be a command, which, of course, we've never given, except in training. But every six weeks we have to have them retrained.

FROST: Gosh, but really he'll give you a warm welcome? It reminds me of the first time I ever earned any money. It was when I was still at school. We always used to do the Christmas postal round—you know people at school did this when they were sixteen. They didn't earn very much money. I delivered the Christmas mail and I always remember going to houses with large dogs.

GRAHAM: I did too.

[16]

FROST: And these dogs would go GRR-R-R and the woman in the background would be yelling, "It's just his way of saying hello." LAUGHTER. You weren't at all sure.

GRAHAM: Well, I used to deliver milk. My father was a dairy farmer and we used to deliver milk early in the morning. I've had some of those experiences that you're talking about so I can sympathize with you. There were several houses we called on in great fear and trembling.

FROST: Yes, and one other thing—it's nothing whatever to do with what we're talking about. What you were saying triggered it off. There was one senior postman in this particular town who was famed for reading the postcards from people abroad. He was the nosiest man imaginable, and he used to come back to the post office and say, "Mrs. Perkins is having a very good time in Sweden. You know, he just read everybody's business when they sent postcards. And then one day, I always remember, he came back in a state of absolute fury and said, "Look at this, look at this." His name was Cheese and someone had written this card from wherever they were abroad, and on the card it said, "Dear Mum, Dad, and Mr. Cheese." LAUGHTER. Absolutely marvelous, he'd been seen through!

GRAHAM: Well, I remember one night about three o'clock in the morning, I was delivering milk. The snow had fallen and the dog got after me in this particular house and I ran in a direction that I had never taken before to get back to the milk truck. A clothes wire had been strung and it caught me right in the neck. I did a double twist and almost severed my head from the body. Then the dog came and attacked me while I was down. I'll never forget that.

[17]

Like David Frost, Billy Graham has a warm relationship with his widowed mother, who lives in the family home in Charlotte, North Carolina.

FROST: Is that when you decided to give up being a milkman?

LAUGHTER

GRAHAM: No, I decided that the first day I had to milk cows. I used to have to milk about twenty cows before I went to school in the morning, all through my high school days. Then I had to milk those same cows when I came home in the afternoon. I decided then that I thought there were other things in life that I could do rather than milking cows. But that's not the reason I went into the ministry. Before I went into the ministry, I had often said that there were two things that I'd never do—one, be an undertaker and the other, be a clergyman. I put them both in the same category.

FROST: Really? When was it, that in order to raise a little money for your studies you were terrific at selling brushes?

GRAHAM: Yes, I sold brushes from door to door in the depression period in the United States to make enough money to help in my schooling. My father helped me, but not enough for all my needs. So I went at it with all the zest that I could and would work from morning to night selling brushes. My technique was to offer the lady a free brush and, of course, in those days that appealed. I would have to empty my whole case of brushes to get to the bottom, you see, to give this free brush LAUGHTER and the woman's curiosity was aroused by looking at the brushes and she would say, "By the way, what is this." "How much is that." Well, I knew I had a fish on the string like that. Many times you'd go to the door and the lady would come and just crack it open. I knew that the door was soon going to slam, so I always put my foot in the door there and would offer her the free brush. "No, I'm not

[19]

here to sell you anything, I'm here to give you a brush." Well, some of the biggest sales were made that way. I never really made big sales where I thought I was going to make them, I always made them in places where the woman said, "no, no, no" in the beginning—always knew that was a good one.

FROST: That was the one that could be convinced in the end. Were any of those techniques of value later in public speaking?

GRAHAM: Oh, I would think so because I was naturally sort of a shy fellow and I didn't particularly like to meet people. That got me over that. It allowed me to talk with people and to sell people. I never took a speech course in my life. I never have read a book on speech. Because the way I speak in the pulpit is my natural form of speaking, except before a big crowd, I speak a bit louder than I do talking to you here.

FROST: Well, we've got to take a break now and who knows what the commercial will be. Maybe it will be for brushes. We'll be right back.

APPLAUSE.

FROST: Welcome back, welcome back. One of the other events of the past few weeks was the Archbishop of Canterbury's visit to South Africa where he had a forty minute face-to-face session with Mr. Vorster, the Prime Minister of South Africa and the prime exponent of its apartheid policies. Everybody described him as emerging visibly shaken. I wonder if you had a forty minute session with Mr. Vorster, would you find that difficult? What do you think you would say to him?

GRAHAM: Well, I suppose I would say approximately what I think the Archbishop said to him. I've been quite happy with

Graham chats with Dr. Arthur Michael Ramsey, the Archbishop of Canterbury (right), and Archbishop Athanasius Y. Samuel, head of the Syrian Antiochian Orthodox Church of North America.

the Archbishop's tour thus far down there. I've never been to South Africa. I've been invited many times but felt that I couldn't go because I have a policy of never preaching to segregated audiences. I wouldn't even want to go and preach in areas where a permit had to be made and an exception made, if you know what I mean, as the Archbishop did. I feel that I have to stand on a little stronger principle than that. But I could understand his position and I've looked on his trip as sort of a John the Baptist thing for me—that someday, if he gets along well and gets through all the pitfalls, I might consider an invitation. I'm told by some of my friends that have been there that the situation has, in some areas, been exaggerated, and that it is possible to hold integrated meetings in South Africa. Now whether that's true or not, I don't know. I intend to correspond with the Archbishop and try to get a private evaluation of his tour and of his reactions. But I don't think anyone anywhere in the world could possibly excuse apartheid. One of the things that disturbs me in the United States at the moment is there's a certain element in the black community—a small element to be sure—that wants separatism in the United States. For example, I know a university where the dormitories are now completely integrated, but where the blacks are saying, "No, we want our own dormitory, we want our own classes, we want separatism." Now whether this is going to be the beginning of something that will grow—I hope not. I think the only hope for America to settle her race problem is an integrated society. But there are those today that don't agree with that, in the black community as well as the white community, and whether they will gain momentum or not, I don't know.

FROST: How do you think the battle against racialism is going?

GRAHAM: I think it's going better in the South than in the North. I believe Martin Luther King was correct when he predicted several years ago that the problem in the South would be solved much before it would be in the North. You see, in the South you have great personal friendships between black and white. The blacks hardly know the whites in the North, except in certain top circles. I have many friends among black people who have moved from the South to the North, and have already moved back because they don't like it in the North. They feel there's a hypocrisy in the North. And we had what was called de jure segregation in the South which has been completely done away with. But we never really faced up to de facto segregation which you have in the northern part of the United States. So I would say that it would be in the major cities of the North where the explosions will come. God forbid that there will be any more. That's why this next year in our crusading, we are concentrating on cities in the North like Cleveland, Chicago, and Oakland, California, where there's been a lot of disturbance and where the headquarters of the Black Panthers are. And we're going to hold crusades in those cities next year, hoping that our meetings may have some healing effect. Because through television and the mass media, and these big crowds, we can say something to a local community.

FROST: You're obviously in a sense saying apartheid is an evil system. Do you believe there is such a thing as the Devil?

GRAHAM: Yes, I definitely do. I think the Bible teaches there is a personality called the Devil, and I think there are millions of demons whose power is growing in the world. Because, as

[23]

James Weston, former member of the Black Panthers, who now directs a Christian ministry in California, converses with Billy Graham at a Congress on Evangelism.

we approach the end of history—not the end of the world, not the end of the human race—but the end of this historical period we call the age of the Spirit of God, I believe that Satan's activities are going to intensify—in violence, in war, and in all the disturbances that we now see taking place in the world. Yes, to answer your question directly, there is a Devil.

FROST: What's he like?

GRAHAM: Well, the Bible tells us quite a bit about him. He's called the Prince of this World, the Prince of the Power of the Air, and the God of this World. He's said to have tremendous power. He doesn't have a body like yours and mine. We can't see him; he's not a fellow with horns and a red suit racing up and down the aisles.

FROST: He isn't?

GRAHAM: You remember the old story, I'm sure—I think it happened here in England—a fellow dressed up in a red suit with horns and a pitchfork came into a little country church on a Sunday morning. Everybody flew out the windows and out the door, they were so frightened. But one lady in the front row remained in the pew. He went up to her with his pitchfork and said, "Aren't you afraid of me?" "Oh," she said, "No sir, Mr. Devil, I've been on your side all the time." LAUGHTER. But, you see, he's not like that. The Bible says that he's a tremendous power, one who led a revolt against God. Apparently when he was banished from Heaven in some mysterious way that I couldn't possibly explain, he landed on this planet and this planet became a planet in rebellion. This is the one planet that God is most concerned about, insofar as we know, in the whole universe. It was to this planet that

[25]

He was willing to send His Son to rescue us from the power of the Devil. That's what the Gospel of Christ is all about. The good news is: God says, "I'll restore you and forgive you and give you strength and power to face life and death."

FROST: Can you think of a moment when you can remember a feeling that the Devil was working on you?

GRAHAM: Yes, definitely. In fact, David, I think people would be rather surprised. I sense it every day, because I'm tempted every day and temptation comes from the Devil. The Bible says God doesn't tempt any man. God will try a person, He will test him, but He doesn't tempt anyone to do evil. That's done by the Devil. And the Devil is constantly after a person like me. I was in France about three weeks ago when the American ambassador entertained us at a little dinner party. There was a very famous French novelist there who came up to me and said, "Mr. Graham, you know, I'm sure, that you are the object of tremendous evil forces. They want to attack you because you are a provocation to evil." And I said, "Yes, I have sensed that;" I have to be very careful in the life I lead, keeping up my defenses by prayer and Bible study, because the Bible says we're not up against flesh and blood—we're up against principalities and powers and forces of wickedness— we're up against a great spiritual force, and when anybody tries to stand up for the Gospel or stand out for good, he's going to be opposed by these evil forces in the world.

FROST: What sort of temptations were you thinking of? What sort of temptations have you felt in the past six weeks?

GRAHAM: Well, the Bible says that Jesus Christ was tempted in all points like as we are, yet without sin. There are three main temptations that man has—there's the lust of the flesh,

[26]

there's the lust of the eye, and there's the pride of life; in other words, ego. All three of these are temptations that Satan brings to us every day, tempting us in a thousand different ways and coming at us from different angles, but always using those three main avenues. This is what he used on Adam and Eve in the Garden of Eden; this is what he used on Jesus in the Mount of Temptation in the wilderness, and he hasn't changed his tactics. His tactics are still the same and man is still falling for the same old arguments.

FROST: Which of the three does he go at you most with?

GRAHAM: All three of them.

FROST: Does he?

GRAHAM: Of course, I'm no exception. I couldn't say that I was better than my Lord, and the Pope would have to say the same. Every one of us will have to confess these things, you see. For example, an evil thought can come to my mind. Now it doesn't become sin, it is not sin to be tempted, unless I yield to the temptation.

FROST: So the thought is not necessarily, it's the commit—

GRAHAM: No, it's the mulling over the thought and sort of going over in my mind—

FROST: The joy of evil, is it?

GRAHAM: Yes, that's right. That's correct, that's the sin. And that's called in the Bible "evil imagination." And that was one of the sins which led to the destruction of the human race when Noah was able to build his ship and escape with his family of eight and the animals.

FROST: Anything more than about seventeen seconds and it starts to . . .LAUGHTER.

GRAHAM: Well, I wouldn't want to put a time limit . . . LAUGHTER.

[27]

FROST: I know you don't drink alcohol, do you at all? Would you classify that as a sin. I mean a lot of Christians drink.

GRAHAM: No, because I don't think that the Bible teaches teetotalism. When the Bible says that Jesus turned water into wine that wasn't grape juice in my judgment; that was wine—the best wine. And I think that the Scripture teaches in the last chapter of Proverbs, for example, that when a person has troubles, and in old age that it's good to take some alcohol. Paul, writing to Timothy says, "Take a little wine for your stomach's sake." You'd be amazed at how many people have stomach trouble and use that to justify it. LAUGHTER. But the reason that I don't drink, David, is because I feel that there is another principle at work. The Bible says if I do anything to make my brother stumble or fall, then I'm not to do it. If people saw me sitting at a table drinking, in America at least, then they might say, "Well, Billy Graham does it; it's all right for me;" and they may become alcoholics as a result of it. So I have to be careful of my witness.

FROST: Well, I was going to say that. I often feel that it's unfair of people to say, "Why does Billy Graham stay in a good hotel?" They write articles like that while living in a good hotel themselves. I think it very unfair of them to demand that you live in different surroundings. I have wondered if in fact there are things like that, that really are innocent pleasures, but, because they might be misinterpreted, you cannot get involved in.

GRAHAM: As you know, I don't get that type of criticism in the United States, but I do when I go to England. Because if I stay, for example, in a top hotel here—there's at least one

hotel here that gives me quite a break financially because it's an American-dominated hotel—I would be criticized. But if I stay in the same chain of hotels in the United States, it's looked upon as normal. That is where a person stays. Now I don't live in a palace, like Lambeth Palace. I don't have my own chauffeur-driven motor car. I don't have all of the things that some bishops and cardinals have, including a lot of servants, but in America I generally stay in a chain called the Holiday Inns. The reason that I stay there is because from the inception, these inns have given me free room and free board for me and my family and my friends who are with me. The same is true at the Marriott Hotels. So I am quite a free-loader. If they'll keep me free, I'll go and enjoy it.
LAUGHTER

FROST: Yes, well I think that people point sometimes, don't they, to the sort of penniless life of Jesus and then say, "Well, why don't his followers today live a similar penniless life? That seems to me—well, I don't wholly sympathize with that point of view because I think times do change. Another thing people point out is that Jesus seemed very much "agin" the system. He was outside of the system, He was opposed to the system, and He was, in a sense, a rebel against the system. You are a great friend of a lot of the men within the system, and again I don't think myself that there's anything wrong with that, but what is your answer to people who say you ought to be "agin" the system, you ought to be . . .

GRAHAM: Well, let's say . . .

FROST: . . . you ought to be like Jesus, not going into the . . .

GRAHAM: Well, I think we have to understand what Jesus was against. He never did say a word against Rome, and Rome

[29]

ruled the world, including the country He came from. He never said a word against Rome. He was against the religious system and He dealt primarily with religious questions. When they tried to trap Him and tried to get Him to say that He gave allegiance to Caesar or He was against Caesar, He said, "Bring me a coin," and asked, "Who's picture's on that," and they said, "Caesar's." He said, "Render unto Caesar the things that are Caesar's and unto God the things that are God's." He made that distinction and He never said anything against Rome. The system He was against was an evil, corrupt, hypocritical religious system. Now I make pretty strong statements against what I believe to be the theological and moral corruption that we have in certain areas of the church today. If I go to some area where the church has not taken a strong stand on the race question, I will criticize that church. And I feel that I am against that part of the religious system, because it was this system really, David, that I think brought about the Communist Revolution of 1918 in the Soviet Union. The religious system had become so tied into the political system, and they were both corrupt, that people wanted a change. This terrific system had become corrupt by 1917 and 1918 in what is now the Soviet Union. I think we must make a distinction between the religious system and the political system. Jesus never said anything against the political system even though it was corrupt. He seemed to think this was outside His jurisdiction.

FROST: We're going to take a break there. In fact we've had a very long session. Coming back to the thing you were saying earlier when we were talking about the Devil and evil, have you ever met anybody who you've thought, "There is an evil man?"

GRAHAM: No, perhaps I'm too easy-going and perhaps I think too well of everybody. I really do love everybody. I have not met anybody that I didn't like and didn't love. And I have seen pictures of Eichmann and Hitler and people like that and I am sure there are thousands like them today who I believe are dominated by evil, a power outside themselves, I've seen some of these people on the screen that I think are dominated by supernatural evil power. In Jesus' day they would call it demon possession.

FROST: But none of them were born evil, you wouldn't have . . .

GRAHAM: Yes, we are all born with a tendency to evil. I mean we all have the seed of evil within us, of hate and lust and greed. And that's called original sin.

FROST: And this is called a break; we'll be right back.

MUSIC, APPLAUSE.

APPLAUSE, MUSIC.

FROST: Welcome back. Billy was about to tell me something as a P.S. to what we were just talking about earlier.

GRAHAM: Oh, a few minutes ago we were talking about whether you live in good hotels and all that sort of thing. I was thinking about an experience when I came over to England in 1954 for a crusade at Harringay Arena and Wembley Stadium. I was asked at a press conference why I didn't travel like Jesus—why would I come on this big beautiful, luxurious Queen Mary. I said, "Well, Jesus traveled on a

[31]

Billy Graham, a frequent visitor at the White House during the Johnson Administration, receives the former President and Mrs. Johnson during a Graham evangelistic crusade in Houston.

donkey. You find me a donkey that can swim the Atlantic and I'll try to buy him. LAUGHTER.

FROST: But no one's come up with one?

GRAHAM: No, I haven't found a donkey that can swim the Atlantic so I'm afraid I'm going to have to continue to use airlines and ships. LAUGHTER.

FROST: I know two of your greatest friends are Lyndon Johnson and Richard Nixon, and indeed you stayed on from one administration to the next, didn't you? LAUGHTER I mean you were staying, wasn't it the week before . . .

GRAHAM: Yes, Mr. Johnson's last weekend, the weekend of the inauguration, my wife and I were his only house guests that weekend. We went to church with him on his last Sunday. And we stayed over and on the Monday morning when Mr. Nixon was inaugurated, I was on the platform and gave the inaugural prayer. A very sweet and wonderful little thing happened to me that I've never heard anybody mention. I was sitting right behind Vice President Humphrey and President Johnson, during the inauguration ceremony. After it was over, Mr. Nixon who was now the president of the United States, left first with his family. As the Johnson family left, Linda, came over to me and kissed me and so did Luci—right on the platform—then walked out with their father and mother. And it's rather sweet, I think, because we were very good friends of the Johnsons and I love the Johnsons very much as people. I think they're a marvelous family and I also think a great deal of the Nixons.

FROST: How would you compare Lyndon Johnson and Richard Nixon as men?

GRAHAM: I think their philosophy is probably much alike. I mean they both, I think, have many things in common but

[33]

*The evangelist chats informally at 1968 Republican Convention
with Tricia and Julie, President Nixon's daughters, and David
Eisenhower, Julie's husband.*

their technique and approach and method is totally different. Mr. Johnson is a great activist and moves things very fast. Mr. Nixon is a great student—he studies and reads and thinks through and takes his actions that are quite deliberate. And I think personally that Richard Nixon is the best trained man that's ever been in the White House. I doubt if we've ever had a man in history that's so prepared himself for the White House. But I think one of the problems he's running into, and any president is going to run into, is that some people think that America may have reached the point where it cannot be governed—the problems are now so overwhelming. As a matter of fact, I said that in my inaugural prayer. *Time* Magazine said that Billy Graham gave his own inauguration address in the prayer. LAUGHTER   I mentioned in the prayer that the problems were almost insoluble and they are. We've brought the best brains—the Democratic party has tried for many years, the Republican party is trying, but the problems are still there, and there doesn't seem to be a solution. I think that Mr. Nixon is right when he says that ours is a spiritual crisis. Unless we have a renewal of the American spirit, which I believe is based upon a religious spirit, I don't think we can solve some of these problems. Look at the economic problem or the race problem or the crime problem or the revolutionary problem or the student problem—all of these are problems that are beyond the ability of a president to cope with. And another thing that's been interesting to me, in knowing these various men, is how limited their power really is. You know we think of a president as being all-powerful. Well, he can push that button in an international war. There's no doubt that in that sense he is powerful. But when it comes to solving these great problems like student unrest, he's extremely limited in power. He can lead, he can influence, but that's about as far as he can go.

FROST: President Nixon in that address talked of bringing us together. How much can a president do in that area, do you think?

GRAHAM: I think he can do a great deal, but I don't think we're going to be brought together quite like that. It seems to me that we've got extremists, David, extreme right and the extreme left, that are almost irreconcilable. And we've got a group of people now that really believe in the violent overthrow of the government. They do not have any system that they would like to substitute, they've come forward with no plan yet; they just want to destroy. And I don't know whether you can carry on a dialogue with this type of person or not. Some of them will talk to me. I have met with them several times. And I just find that it's almost impossible to reason with them. They're not interested in reason; they're not interested in dialogue; they're not interested in sitting down quietly and talking about the problem. They're interested in disruption, in violence, in destruction, to bring down the system.

FROST: And given that there are, you know, a really violent fringe at each end, if you know what I mean—really violent . . .

GRAHAM: Right . . .

FROST: But then if you come in a little from that to people like Hardhats and, on the other hand, you know students who are protesting against the system, passionately, but not violently, how do you bring those two groups together? I

[36]

President and Mrs. Richard M. Nixon are shown with the popular evangelist, during a Graham campaign in Knoxville, Tennessee.

know you'll never bring a Ku Klux Klan man together with a really violent Weatherman—you know what I mean—but how do you bring closer together a right wing Hardhat and a left wing student?

GRAHAM: Well, you mean that middle silent majority?

FROST: Well, no, I just meant those two opposing groups . . .

GRAHAM: I would say . . .

FROST: . . . leaving aside the very violent fringe who obviously you're never going to bring together.

GRAHAM: I would doubt that we could ever get them to agree, but maybe we can get them to work for change within the system. I don't think there's ever been a system devised that's absolutely perfect in history. I don't think we've ever had a Utopian situation in world history though America probably has come close to it. I think the British have come as close to it, but no system has been perfect. We all know there's a need for change in the educational system, and there's a need for social justice. We shouldn't have ghettos in modern America. They should be eliminated. But can we bring this about within the constitution, within the framework of government, rather than tearing the whole thing down, having total chaos followed by a dictatorship taking over? That's exactly what would happen. If we destroy the system, a dictator is going to rise—either a right-winger or a left-winger.

FROST: We're going to take a break there, we'll be right back with Billy Graham.

APPLAUSE, MUSIC.

MUSIC, APPLAUSE.

FROST: I was talking to somebody the other day and they

[38]

were saying that they saw you with your wife recently—which is not surprising. I don't mean it was an event or anything . . .

GRAHAM: Yes, I'm with her from time to time.

FROST: Right, and they'd just been married themselves, and they said that you and your wife were a terrific example to them on how to stay in love when you've been married for some years. What would you say makes a marriage work?

GRAHAM: I think to have a successful marriage you need two very good forgivers. They have to learn to forgive each other, and I think the most difficult period of marriage is probably the first five years of adjustment. That's very difficult. After about five years, there develops an understanding so that a couple can communicate with each other without ever saying a word. I know that in my own case, I suppose it's been at least fifteen years since my wife and I have had a cross word between us. We think alike, we believe alike, and we desperately love each other. I love her far more now than I did when I married her, and I know she loves me. We have learned to accept the faults of the other. I think that Abraham Lincoln was right when he said, I've learned to accept the faults of my friends. I think you can establish a friendship or marriage relationship when you learn to realize that no one is perfect, that we do have little faults; and then thirdly, I think there must be spiritual affinity. There must be something more than the physical or the material. There must be a spiritual understanding in a marriage, and if there isn't this spiritual oneness and understanding, I think the marriage is in danger. It must have a strong rock upon which to build, and of course, when two people can face a problem and can pray about it and talk about it in a spiritual dimension and face it that way, the possibility of settling that problem is far greater.

FROST: Do you have much sympathy with the Womens' Liberation Movement in the States?

GRAHAM: Well, in the December issue of the *Ladies Home Journal* I had several thousand words on the subject LAUGHTER and I suppose that I'm going to get a lot of letters on my article, because after I wrote the article, I submitted it to my wife, because she's a marvelous critic. She handed it back to me all blue-penciled and said, "I don't agree with most of this." So I re-wrote it. So what I have written is partially what my wife believes. I said that I felt that woman didn't have much of a chance in the world till Jesus came along, that the liberation He gave was a liberation of the spirit. Some of the extremists in the Womens Lib. Movement are almost wanting to take away childbearing and motherhood from women. Man is going to have a hard time maintaining the population.

FROST: On his own.

GRAHAM: On his own. I don't think the average man could have a baby. LAUGHTER

FROST: So that, in general, you think they're missing the point a bit?

GRAHAM: Yes, I think so. I believe that when it comes to equal pay for equal work, they have a big point and I'm in sympathy with them. But some of these other rather ridiculous things! One group said that they wanted even the signs on the rest rooms taken down. You see, that was discrimination. Well, to go to that ridiculous extreme is against human nature. It's against everything that man is inside.

FROST: It would lead to a great deal of consternation.

GRAHAM: Exactly.

FROST: That's a fascinating point. You mentioned love just now naturally when talking about marriage. What would be— I've asked a lot of people this—your definition of love between a man and a woman?

GRAHAM: I think the love between a man and a woman is described very accurately by the Apostle Paul in the thirteenth chapter of I. Corinthians, in which he says that love is patient, love never gets angry, and love does not hold grudges. I believe that in order to have successful married love, we have to work at it. You know, we've got the idea that love is some sort of sensual feeling, or we've got the idea that love is something that sort of hits you. I'm convinced that love grows. I'm sure that when I got married, I didn't really love my wife in the depths that I'm able to love her now, or that she loves me. We called it love, but there's a great gap between that little puppy love that we started with and what I believe to be a gigantic Rock of Gibraltar love that we have now. But that's taken work.

FROST: What's the difference between that love—your love for your wife, and your love for your children or your love for your God? How do they differ?

GRAHAM: There are three words in Greek that are translated "love." One is eros, which is sensuous love; another is friendship love, the type of love that I would have for a friend. And finally there is agape love, and that love is God's kind of love. The New Testament writers had to invent a brand new word. It did not previously exist in Greek. This new word is used to

[41]

Billy Graham never fails to give high praise to his wife, Ruth, for her influence on his ministry. Here they walk hand in hand in the fields near their home.

describe God's love, total love, God's love for us even when we were sinners and rebellious against Him. He loved us so much that He gave His Son to die on the cross for us. That's God's love. Now the moment I received Christ as my Savior, God gave me the gift of that love. I have an ability to love supernaturally so that the love that I have in my marriage—between two Christians—is the love that is a supernatural love. There's a depth to it—a joy to it—there's an excitement, even an ecstasy, that I don't think a person outside of God knows about.

FROST: That's a terrific added advertisement for Christianity.

GRAHAM: Well, I think it's definitely true.

FROST: Human relationships that are superhuman in a way.

GRAHAM: I think that is so.

FROST: We'll take a break there. We'll be right back.

MUSIC, APPLAUSE.

APPLAUSE, MUSIC

FROST: Welcome back, welcome back. Christmas is getting very close. How are you planning to splend—spend or splend whatever that means LAUGHTER, how are you planning to splend lis Chlismas? LAUGHTER   That's for our Chinese listeners.

GRAHAM: This year's going to be a little bit different from what we've spent in other years. We have to leave the day after Christmas to go to California where Ruth and I are the grand marshall of the Rose Parade. This means that we're going to have to hurry Christmas along. We'll have a lot of our family with us—we hope all of our family, and then we're going to put them all in a plane and take the whole crowd

[43]

out to California where we will be involved in about a week-long series of festivities, climaxing with the Rose Parade, and the Rose Bowl. And so I have done most of my Christmas shopping in two hours at one of the stores in London, while I was here, and . . .

FROST: The same store that I do my Christmas (blip) in . . .
LAUGHTER.

GRAHAM: And I bought all of my children little presents and bought my wife a couple of things. I would tell you what I bought her but she might see this before Christmas so I can't reveal it. LAUGHTER. But I did have a good time doing this Christmas shopping. Christmas Eve we always hang up stockings for everybody and we put our presents in them. Then we gather and have hymn singing and carol singing and prayers. We have prayers every evening in our home. Then Christmas morning we get up rather early, keeping the tradition of the little children, when they used to wake us up early. We have oyster stew for some strange reason. My wife and I are about the only two that seem to like it. LAUGHTER. She wrote a book one time on Christmas and she wrote that we always did this on Christmas Day so she has to keep it up every year even though very few of the family like it. LAUGHTER. Then for Christmas dinner we always have the traditional turkey, and in the afternoon we try to sort of sleep it off.

FROST: What the oyster stew mainly? LAUGHTER

GRAHAM: That's right. The oyster stew is beginning to gurgle a bit by that time and the oysters are swimming about. But seriously, Christmas to us is not much of a commercial thing. It's a family occasion and it's a time when we try to remember, very seriously, what Christmas is all about. A lot of people forget that.

[44]

Part of the Graham family on the grounds of their mountain-top home at Montreat, North Carolina. Left to right: Graham's youngest son Ned, Dr. Graham, Bunny (now Mrs. Theodore Dienert), Franklin, and Mrs. Ruth Graham.

FROST: The great message of Christmas is always peace on earth, good will to men. And when you predict that the end of this period of human history, or the end of the world, is close, do you think that peace on earth is impossible?

GRAHAM: Well you see, the peace that Christ really came to bring was personal peace—peace of the individual in the midst of turmoil and in a frustrated, confused, warring world. "My peace I give unto you," He said. Also He came to bring peace on earth—in the sense of peace with God. This planet is looked upon in the Bible as at war with God. He came to bring peace between man and God. Then, thirdly, He came to bring ultimate peace. There is going to be peace on earth. I mean we're going to have world peace. There's no doubt about it, but it's not going to be brought about by Mr. U Thant in the United Nations. They're going to try, and they can patch it up here and there, but it's going to break out all over. The only permanent peace the world will ever know is when God intervenes in human history and Jesus Christ is put on the throne. He's going to rule and reign and we're going to have peace. But He will rule with a rod of iron the Bible says, and that is when death will be eliminated, suffering will be eliminated, poverty eliminated.

FROST: Last time, at the first coming of Christ, He came to Palestine. Is there any indication to which country He might come next?

GRAHAM: Oh yes, the fourteenth chapter of Zechariah tells us exactly where He's coming.

FROST: Well, I've forgotten the fourteenth chapter.
LAUGHTER.

Billy Graham is a strong believer in physical fitness. Here he jogs on the beach with son-in-law Ted Dienert, a Philadelphia advertising agency executive.

GRAHAM: He's going to come to the Mount of Olives. He's going to stand on the Mount of Olives, the Bible says, and Jerusalem will become the capital of the world, and from Jerusalem, Christ is going to reign.

FROST: Well, we've got that sorted out.

GRAHAM: We'd better not go into the question of Jerusalem today. That's a political question.

FROST: Well, I was just thinking about Jerusalem today and a conversation I had with a marvelous man, the Mayor of Jerusalem, doing his best to bring the peoples together. We must take a break though, we're drawing to the end of the program, but we're not quite there I'm glad to say, we'll be right back with Billy Graham.

MUSIC, APPLAUSE.

APPLAUSE, MUSIC

FROST: Welcome back. There've been a lot of questions in the past hour, Billy, and I know you're a man of great intellectual curiosity yourself. Eventually, when this life is over—many, many years from now because you look younger every time I meet you—you eventually go to Heaven and . . .

GRAHAM: That's the make-up that gives me my disguise
LAUGHTER

FROST: Oh is it? No, it isn't. I saw you without make-up as well. But when you eventually meet God face to face is there a question you'll want to ask Him?

GRAHAM: Yes, I think so. I'm going to ask, "Lord, why did you choose me to do this particular work?" Because I've never really understood how I was chosen to go around the world preaching to these great crowds of people and I'm

[48]

humbled by it and honored by it. But it's not the life I personally would have chosen. I think it was chosen by God who gave me this privilege and this opportunity. I want to ask Him why, when there are so many wonderful people in the world that are His servants, He chose me.

MUSIC

FROST: If he hadn't chosen you—that's the end of our time, I'm sure—but if he hadn't chosen you to be an evangelist, what might you have chosen to be? Not a milkman, we know that from the beginning. What other profession?

GRAHAM: I probably would have gone into politics. Politics fascinates me.

FROST: We'll talk about that next time. Thank you very much.

MUSIC, APPLAUSE

[49]

Telecast from New York

FROST: And now it's my great joy and privilege to welcome a friend who really needs no introduction. Will you welcome, please, Dr. Billy Graham.

APPLAUSE.

So good to see you here.

GRAHAM: Well, thank you, David, and thank you for that warm welcome.

FROST: Well, it's very, very good that you're able to join us. I'm delighted. I was delighted, too, to read that the crusade recently at Madison Square Garden went so well.

GRAHAM: Well it did. It was a bit of a surprise to us because we had it on television three times a day in New York, and at night at prime time. We had it throughout the Eastern seaboard and we thought that being live on television, or delayed an hour or two would cut our audience down, but it seemed to work the other way. I was quite surprised because the Garden was jammed to capacity and overflowing every night except one, when there was a rainstorm. But it was really a tremendous reception and so overwhelming that

[51]

there's a great deal of talk about the possibility of coming back next year to the Garden and keeping our organization intact very much as we did in London.

FROST: You mean in '54 and '55?

GRAHAM: Well, '54 and '55 and then '66 and '67.

FROST: Right. Tell me—that raises the subject that I think is one of the many interesting things about you, which is, at root, what is the gift, what is it that you've got that other preachers haven't?

GRAHAM: Well, I think, David, that God gave me the gift of an evangelist. The Bible teaches that there's the gift of the pastor, there's the gift of the teacher, and there's the gift of an evangelist. Now, the church through the years, in my judgment, has neglected the gift of the evangelist. And yet that is a gift that God gives to certain people. You've had them in Britain—men like George Whitefield and John Wesley, and the great evangelists who have had a great impact in the United States. America owes more to those evangelists than our historians have ever given them credit for.

FROST: What is it that makes you then a bigger evangelist than anybody else?

GRAHAM: Well . . .

FROST: What is the gift? What is it?

GRAHAM: Well, let's say that I'm not bigger, perhaps, in God's sight, but maybe in the sight of a newspaper or television station; because we have electronics today, the electronic medium of television. The average life span of an evangelist at his peak performance has been about ten years because they used to preach to huge crowds without amplification. Well, I not only have amplification, but I have television and radio

*Huge throngs are attracted to Billy Graham's meetings every-
where in the world. Here is a capacity crowd in the new Madison Square Garden, New York.*

and all of these different things that have maintained my ministry over a long period of time.

FROST: But still nobody else has done it the way you have. Certainly there are other evangelists, and there's radio and television. Why again have you made a bigger impact? What is the gift, particularly, you've got?

GRAHAM: Well, that's what I'm saying. I believe it's a gift of the Spirit of God. And when we get to heaven I'm going to reach over and grab David Frost, if you're there . . .

FROST: Thank you, thank you.

GRAHAM: . . . and I'll take you up to the Lord and I'll say, "Now David wants an answer to this question." Actually, I cannot answer your question. I'm as surprised as anyone else that so many people come to my meetings. And I think the reason is—in part at least—that the world in which we're living is so uncertain, with all of its frustration and confusion. People read the tragic story of Judy Garland, for example, splashed all over the papers. And many people say, "Well that is my story. I haven't yet gone that far, but that is the direction I'm taking. I need something."

And I have become a symbol to many of these people that perhaps they can find in a spiritual experience with Christ the answer to their problems.

FROST: And I know one thing—I'm going to knock at the gates of heaven and say, "Billy said I could come in."

GRAHAM: That won't do you any good. You've got to say, "Christ said I could come in."

FROST: You've turned it to a good point there, yes. Tell me, this is a thing that fascinates people, I think, who would like to believe, or believe a bit, or believe there is a God, but

[54]

don't believe there's a personal God. You were saying about your gift, how can you say when you really feel God's helping you? I mean when do you feel that actually feel that, the most?

GRAHAM: I feel it the most, David, when I'm quoting Scripture, or when I'm reading the Bible. Because I believe that the Bible is a living Word, I believe there's supernatural power in those pages. And I believe that the quoted Word of God is a sword in my hand. And if I stick to the Bible and preach the principles and the teachings of the Bible, and quote the Bible, it has its own impact.

Many people who are converted to Christ in our meetings forget everything that I've ever said. My logic doesn't mean a thing to them. They say some of the things I say don't have much logic. But it's the quoted Word of God they can't get away from.

I know a professor at one of our great universities who was converted to Christ. All he could remember after the service was that, "If thou shalt confess with thy mouth the Lord Jesus and believe in thine heart that God hath raised him from the dead, thou shalt be saved." That kept going over and over and over in his mind. He had come to the meeting an agnostic—a British professor who now is a professor in the United States. But he couldn't get over that verse of Scripture.

FROST: Would you give a specific example of the most touching or moving demonstration of faith that you've ever witnessed? One incident that you'd pick and say, "Now that is faith."

GRAHAM: Well, I have had many such incidents happen in my

[55]

The evangelist listens to a bearded youth at a Miami rock festival where Dr. Graham advised young people to get "high" on God instead of on drugs.

life. And there are numerous occasions that have come up. But to say which is the most moving—one could take a small experience or one could take a large experience.

FROST: One of each.

GRAHAM: Well, I remember, for example, the opening night of our meeting in London in '54, which you certainly remember. All the press was against us—every newspaper. The church leaders who had brought us there—many of them had deserted us. It had been brought up in Parliament as to whether I should even be allowed to land in Britain or not. And everything seemed against us.

That afternoon I had invited Senator Stuart Symington and another United States senator to be my guests there. That afternoon Senator Symington called me on the phone and said the American ambassador felt that because of all this bad publicity that he and his colleague should not attend the opening service. "So we have decided not to come," he said. "We're going to have dinner this evening with Sir Anthony Eden." He was then the foreign secretary.

I was called about a half an hour before the service in my little hotel. They said, "The arena is empty. There are four hundred newspaper people here taking pictures of the empty seats." And we had rented Harringay Arena for three months. My wife and I got down on our knees and prayed, "Now, Lord, we're prepared for anything you want. It can be a total flop, or it can be a success. We leave it in your hands." I had great peace about it. It was an exercise in faith to even go out to the arena.

We went out there but didn't see a person. We got out of the car and one of my associates came out of the door behind the arena and said, "Billy, the place is packed, and there are five thousand people on the other side trying to beat the doors down." And I said, "Where did they come from?" They said, "We don't know. God must have sent them." And we were there for three months. Not only did we not have empty seats, but we had two and three services a night on some nights to take care of the people. And ended up at Wembley Stadium with the press all for us, and the Archbishop of Canterbury sitting by my side.

FROST: And a souvenir edition of the *London Evening News*.

GRAHAM: That's right.

FROST: The Billy Graham Edition.

GRAHAM: That is correct. The thing had completely changed. And even the *Daily Mirror's* Cassandra, Bill Connor, who died recently, had become a warm friend. He was now giving us wonderful write-ups, whereas before he had used his pen to tear us apart.

FROST: That's a big example. Now take one small personal example of faith in action, or someone with a touching faith. Can you?

GRAHAM: Well, one night in Los Angeles I was told that one of the leading criminals of this country was in the audience. And they said, "We don't know why he's here. He may be against you, or he may be here out of curiosity. We don't know why he's here." But the men on my committee were trembling. We had a small tent, and were preaching there on a street corner, really.

That night this fellow was asked by an usher if he wanted to go forward when I gave the invitation. He said, "If you speak to me again, I'll take my fist and knock you down."

[58]

But after about a minute or two, suddenly for some un- known reason, he decided to come forward.

Still, everybody in town thought this was a big hoax and a big fraud, and that it would never last. But I talked to him personally and I believed he was sincere. He said, "I want you to go see my boss." His boss was Mickey Cohen, the great West Coast underworld figure. I went out with him to see Mickey Cohen. I don't think Cohen had ever met a clergyman before. He was very nervous and he said, "What do you want to drink?" He repeated, "What does a person like you drink?" I said, "Well give me a Coca Cola." And so he brought me a Coca Cola and we talked for quite a while.

Well, the man who made the decision for Christ, who was working with Mickey Cohen, thought he was going to get it because he had told Cohen that he was going to change his way of living, that he was going straight and going clean. Twenty years later that fellow is doing social work in the City of New York and is one of the great Christian leaders of this city. And his name is Jim Vaus, known to many people.

And the act of faith is this: very few clergymen, very few people had any confidence in the commitment he had made. They thought he was just too bad to ever change. He never turned back one single day. He has lived it, and is now mak- ing a positive contribution here in East Harlem for the work of God—and for social improvement and betterment of this city.

FROST: That's a marvelous example. There's a lot more I want to ask you about. We've got to take a break here, Billy. We'll be back in two minutes time.

[59]

FROST: Tell me, as you look back over your life, are there any of the earlier statements that you made that, as you look back, you grin a little indulgently and they make you blush a little?

GRAHAM: Yes, there are many statements, David, I wish I had never made. And I think this happens to everyone later in life because you become, I hope, more mature and one learns a bit. And in one's travels and contacts and reading one learns. For example, I made the statement many years ago of the actual dimensions of heaven.

FROST: Sixteen hundred miles in each direction.

GRAHAM: You have a very good memory. I didn't know you knew that I made it! And many statements like that were rather foolish that I made and I wouldn't make them today.

FROST: And you made them then because you thought that it was possible to actually know more detailed things than is possible now, or what?

GRAHAM: Well the Bible actually does say how long the new Jerusalem is going to be, sixteen hundred furlongs. But I'm rather inclined to think that's symbolic language whereas I took it more literally, then. Now that doesn't mean that I've changed my mind about the Bible being totally and completely inspired of God. But I do know that the Bible has symbolic language—a great deal of symbolic language.

FROST: How has your actual faith itself developed or changed? I mean, you do stress the details of hell less, for instance, than you once did, don't you?

GRAHAM: Yes, I would think that's true, because I used to use a great deal of imagination, as I think many evangelists like Jonathan Edwards and others did, on the subject of hell.

[60]

Now I just stick to the words of Jesus, and I don't go any further, and I don't try to explain it any more than He explained it. Because there are certain mysteries about heaven and hell, and sin—there are certain mysteries beyond which I don't believe that I'm free to speculate about.

I used to speculate about it. I don't speculate any more. I have complete confidence that God is just, and that God is love, that God is merciful and that God is not going to make any mistakes.

FROST: Well, I know you don't speculate about heaven. I was worried about the way you withdrew your assurance that I'd be there. But how do you think that, for instance, people should view the entry into heaven? I know that they should view it in terms of having accepted Christ, as you would say. But I mean, in the sense that if you take on the one hand, some of the great, late saints and preachers—John Wesley will do as an example, or Martin Luther King, who would obviously go to heaven, and you would think probably that someone like Adolph Hitler would not go to heaven, would go to hell. But, I mean, take someone who's more in the middle, say someone like Joseph Stalin, for instance, what will decide where he will go? Where is he?

GRAHAM: Well.... AUDIENCE LAUGHTER David, first of all, only God could answer that question. I'm not God and I'm not assigning this one to heaven and that one to hell. All I'm doing...

FROST: Good thing I never rode with him.

GRAHAM: All you'd want to do there would be to interview him on your show. That would be quite an achievement, if you could do that.

[61]

FROST: Live by satellite.

GRAHAM: Live by satellite. But I do believe, though that . . .
we smile about it and we laugh about it, but this is really a
serious subject. We face death every day. We see it in the
papers—people dying, people that we see on the screens later
in their motion pictures, although we know they're dead
now.

And we have tried, in this generation, in my judgment, to
suppress death like the nineteenth century people tried to
suppress sex. We today are in the process of suppressing dis-
cussions of death and life after death.

That night that we watched and saw that terrible spectacle
of Senator Bobby Kennedy on the floor of the Ambassador
Hotel, lying there in a pool of blood. And we saw this fellow
that carried dishes come and put a religious object in his
hand. And they say that the last conscious thing that Bobby
Kennedy ever did was to close his hand.

Now the thing that meant more to Senator Kennedy at
that moment was not the fact that he had just won the
California primary—not the fact that he had prominence and
wealth and power. It was his relationship to God and it was
the fact that he was staring eternity in the face.

And yet, we don't prepare for it. How many universities
today take up the subject of death and life after death as
something to be discussed? If you listen, though, to the folk
music that our young people are singing—a lot of it's about
death. Our young people want to know about it, but we're
not telling them anything about it. We're trying to suppress
it. And I think we ought to bring it out in the open. I think
sex ought to be in the open for discussion. I think they've

[62]

gone too far in performance.

FROST: For discussion.

GRAHAM: Right, for discussion. And I think that the matter of death ought to be discussed. How many television shows do you ever watch in which death is discussed and what happens after death?

Now I believe, to answer your question specifically, that there is an actual, literal heaven. I believe there's an actual, literal hell. Don't ask me where and don't ask me what it's going to look like and all of that. I don't know. I only know that Jesus warned us about one and told us of the joys and the happiness of the other.

FROST: Is there any sort of material example you could give of what heaven would be like? I mean, people sometimes talk about paradise and they say it's like a beautiful piece of music by Beethoven. Is there any symbol that you can use?

GRAHAM: Well, a lot of people don't like Beethoven. And I think that everything for our personal happiness will be there. And the Scripture says a very interesting thing—that we're going to serve Him. We're not just going to sit down under a palm tree and have a pretty girl wave a palm leaf over us, as . . .

FROST: That's definitely out . . .

GRAHAM: And we're going to serve . . .

FROST: That would attract me about it.

GRAHAM: We're going to work there. Now maybe that wouldn't attract you, but with all you're doing I'd rather think it might. Because there's going to be plenty of work. And when you think of the fact that there are 100 billion galaxies outside of our own galaxy, there's plenty of room up

[63]

At a presidential prayer breakfast in Washington, Graham is shown with the late President Kennedy.

there for a lot of work and a lot of achievement. And I think we're going to be a marvelous world in the future.

FROST: Where is hell? What are the people in hell going to do?

GRAHAM: Well, I don't know. I don't ever expect to find out. But I'll tell you this. I deserve judgment and I deserve hell because of my sin. Because all of us are sinners—we're rebels against God. I'm going to be in heaven. And the password to heaven is going to be the grace of God, the fact that God loves and He says, "I give you eternal life as a gift, it's free." And I'm going there by the grace of God in Christ.

FROST: You say in the big theological sense we're all sinners— in that sense of being a sinner. Can you think back, in addition to that, to little sins, to the day when you borrowed some candies from a store when you weren't supposed to? Or can you think of other little sins?

GRAHAM: Of course, I mean all of us can. I thought of a time, right now as you said that, when I told my father a lie. That's always bothered me. In fact, it's bothered me very much, because it was quite a big lie.

FROST: Really?

GRAHAM: And this was before my conversion to Christ. And I can think of all kinds of little things. Now they would be little things compared to today's things. But this is not what God is alarmed about, or what the Bible is about.

FROST: No?

GRAHAM: Those are only symptoms of a disease that's deep inside. The real disease is a disease of blood pollution that we call sin.

FROST: What was the lie you told your father?

GRAHAM: Well, I'd rather not tell.

[65]

FROST: We'll take a break there, and we'll see if we can persuade him. We'll be back in two minutes time.

FROST: When we went off the air Billy had a very good reason why he didn't want to say what the lie was. Which was?

GRAHAM: Well, I said that this show appears where my mother lives, and I wouldn't want her to hear the answer.

AUDIENCE REACTION

FROST: Your answer is totally accepted. Earlier on you were talking seriously about Senator Kennedy. You, of course, are linked at the moment, in people's minds, with the advice and the friendship you give to many political leaders. Do you like to feel, in a sense, that you can have some influence on political leaders? Or would you rather have none?

GRAHAM: Well, what has happened is that I have been friends with two or three men who became President years later—after our friendship began. I knew Mr. Johnson for many years and I knew Mr. Nixon for many years. I knew his father and mother as far back as 1949. And then he became Senator after that, and then Vice President. And through the years our friendship grew.

And he has told me many times, "Billy, at all costs, you stay out of politics." And in 1960, he said, when there was some pressure on me to endorse him, and I had no intention of getting into politics if I could avoid it, but he told me at that time, he said, "Your ministry is more important than my election." And this has been his attitude.

And he would never, never try to use me politically. And neither did President Johnson. President Johnson called me the other day and asked me to come down to the ranch and

[66]

Billy Graham, an ardent golfer, addresses the ball on a putt in a game with the famed professional golfer, Arnold Palmer.

Former President Lyndon B. Johnson bows with Billy Graham at a presidential prayer breakfast in a Washington hotel.

spend a weekend with him—my wife and me, which we intend to do. And I have maintained friendships in both parties.

And when I was invited to lead a prayer last summer at the Republican Convention, which got a lot of publicity, people thought that maybe I was swinging to the Republicans. What they didn't know was that I had been invited to lead a prayer first at the Democratic Convention and I had accepted only if the Republicans invited me, so that I could be non-partisan. But, because of all the troubles in Chicago, my little prayer was soon lost in the shuffle.

And so I don't think people even knew I was in Chicago. But they did know that I was in the quietness of Miami Beach.

FROST: That's fascinating. You've said about the ranch—you've said on one occasion that really to know President Johnson you had to see him in those surroundings.

GRAHAM: Yes, President Johnson, in my judgment, had one difficulty and that was that he didn't come over on television like he does in person. In person, he's one of the most persuasive, charming men I have ever known. But that doesn't somehow come over on television. Now whether some of his managers and handlers kept him from this or not, I don't know. But he is a tremendous person, an overwhelming person. He could walk in this room and you'd be conscious of his presence. He has a tremendous presence about him. And people didn't get that idea about him.

FROST: President Nixon, on one occasion publicly gave you part credit for persuading him to run again, didn't he? I saw it quoted in two places.

[69]

GRAHAM: Yes. I don't know whether he did or whether somebody misquoted him. I've never really discussed it with him. But when he was trying to make up his mind whether or not to run, he invited me to come down to Florida and spend a few days with him. I was in bed with pneumonia. And he said, "Come down and breathe some of this good air and sunshine, and we'll have some talk."

So I went down and stayed with him, and we discussed many things and watched a football game. And so I gave him the reasons why I thought any prominent American, in whom many people had confidence, ought to offer himself at a critical period in history. Not specifically him, but any American. And so that was more or less the way we left it. Whether that had any influence in his decision or not, I don't really know, because he's never told me.

FROST: I've read several accounts of your involvement in the choice of Vice President Agnew. What's the truth about that?

GRAHAM: Well the *New York Times* has carried the truth about that.

FROST: Advertisements in the *New York Times?*

GRAHAM: Yes, in June they carried a story in their magazine section on me, and they were accurate at this point. I went up that evening after Mr. Nixon's nomination to congratulate him at his hotel. And he said, "We're going to talk about the Vice President which is a very important decision to make tonight." And he said, "I think you'd find it interesting to listen."

So I went in the room with those Republican leaders. And I must confess I felt a little ill at ease, but I was interested.

[70]

Billy Graham prays with the leaders of both major U.S. political parties. This unusual shot shows him with President Nixon at Graham's crusade in Knoxville, Tenn.

Also, anyone would be curious to hear how these things are done. Mr. Nixon went right around the room and asked every one of the leaders to give his position. And did you know that I never heard the name Agnew mentioned all evening, never heard it mentioned except by one person, A New Yorker. And he was not recommending him. And I certainly never heard Senator Thurmond mention his name, though some people have said he was the one who chose him. That's not true at all. When this was done, and how it was done, I don't know. It was certainly done after four o'clock in the morning when I left, and the others left. I don't know how that came about and I've never asked the President how it came about.

FROST: But that evening the President asked you your view didn't he?

GRAHAM: Yes, he turned to me last and asked me my view. And I felt at that time that he needed a balance to the ticket, and I gave him a recommendation, which, of course, everybody knows he didn't take.

FROST: The recommendation was Mark Hatfield.

GRAHAM: Senator Mark Hatfield, yes, because Senator Hatfield is a very dedicated Christian and holds different views on some issues than Mr. Nixon. I thought it might give balance to the ticket. But, of course, Mr. Nixon is a much wiser man than I am politically and he was certainly apparently right. And Vice President Agnew is, from all I can read and gather, making a great Vice President.

FROST: We're talking about Presidents and the tremendous powers that they hold, and so on. But in a sense, there's almost a sense in which your being off form one day, let's

[72]

say, must be more terrifying almost to you than being off form to a President, or say, being off form to a football player. In a sense, when you go out there to preach, you feel that there are people who are out there whose lives are there to be saved forever. And in a sense, if you're off form, ten people's souls, might be lost forever, who if you were on form, might be saved forever. Isn't that a terrifying experience?

GRAHAM: No, because I don't think of it in those terms, David. It's the content of the message that counts—not whether I'm good or bad, or whether I'm feeling good or bad. It's not that at all. It's not the same as a show you may put on, or someone else may put on. Because I believe that while I'm speaking another voice is speaking. And I depend totally and completely on that other voice, which I believe to be the Holy Spirit applying my message.

FROST: Then if it doesn't matter whether you're on form or off form, why bother? Go to the other extreme, does it matter whether you speak well or badly?

GRAHAM: Well, it does to me. First of all, I want the content to be accurate, I want it to be biblical, and I want it to be simple. And I study and work to make my talk simple, because it's so easy as one goes along, as one studies and reads more and contacts people, to tend to leave the people behind. I study to be simple. The average American has the intelligence of a twelve-year-old: religiously. And so I try to speak to everyone in a sense as though they're children when it comes to religion. And they listen. And I think this is one of the great faults in the pulpit today. This is why people sort of nod and go to sleep when the preacher's preaching— because he's over their heads.

[73]

The late Karl Barth, famous Swiss theologian, poses with Billy Graham after the distinguished professor had delivered a lecture at Princeton (N. J.) Theological Seminary.

FROST: At the same time—it's a controversial thought—obviously some people say, you make it too simple.

GRAHAM: When Dr. Karl Barth, the great Swiss theologian— the greatest theologian of his generation—was visiting America a couple of years ago, he was at one of our great seminaries. A student asked him the question, "Dr. Barth, what is the greatest single thought that ever crossed your mind?" He bowed his head and puffed on his pipe and he slowly lifted his shaggy head, and they thought some tremendous statement was coming forth. They were all on the edge of their seats, when he said, "Jesus loves me, that I know, for the Bible tells me so." Now that's profound, but it is very simple. I think this was the secret of the teaching of Jesus. He talked to people who were illiterate, but they understood him. He used little stories—everyday happenings to illustrate great spiritual truths. He made it so simple that the illiterate people could understand him and I think this is the kind of preaching and teaching we need today in the field of religion.

FROST: Well, this is simple, but not very profound. We'll be back in two minutes.

FROST: Billy, I know that material possessions don't matter too much to you. But if a burglar were to get into your house somehow, and he told you he'd leave you one material possession or gift, if you asked him nicely, what would you say you wanted to keep?

GRAHAM: My wife. I hope she's watching.

LAUGHTER, APPLAUSE

FROST: And we hope that your mother's not watching and that your wife is watching.

[75]

GRAHAM: Yes, but my mother doesn't live with me, you see.

FROST: That's a marvelous answer. Would it all have been possible without your wife, do you think?

GRAHAM: No. My wife, David—you must know David and I have been friends for a number of years and that's why we call each other David and Billy—you must know her because she is an unusual person. She rarely ever shows temperament. Her disposition is the same all the time—very sweet and very gracious and very charming and she is a great student of the Bible. Her life is ruled by the Bible more than any person I've ever known. That's her rule book, her compass, and she reared our children—our five children—with the Bible in one hand and a switch in the other. And they turned out pretty well.

FROST: Did she use the Bible a bit more than the switch?

GRAHAM: She used the Bible more than the switch. That's correct.

FROST: In terms of instructing people, is there a commandment that you would add to the Ten in the Old Testament and the two in the New Testament? Do you think today we need any new commandments?

GRAHAM: No. That's the total law right there. I think Christ said that the summation of the total law was to love the Lord thy God with all thy heart, mind and soul and thy neighbor as thyself. But, I think, though, that our problem comes in theology, if I may digress for a moment. Jesus put it right. I must have a vertical relationship with God before I can have an adequate relationship with my fellow man, because from God I get the power to love my fellow man as I should. A lot of what we call love today isn't really love. There is a lot of selfishness in modern love. And the love that God gives is totally unselfish.

FROST: Does your life as a leader—a religious leader—become a lonely one at times? You once talked about the Pope's life being a lonely life. Is your life lonely in some ways?

GRAHAM: I would think that from a human point of view, it would be to the average person, but not to me. Because to a Christian who really believes in God and believes that Christ dwells in him and he has a Bible or a Testament that he carries around to study or read as though God were talking to him, there's no loneliness, there's no boredom. And that's why a person like Paul could be imprisoned in the Mamertine jail in Rome and write a letter to the Philippians and use the word "joy" time after time and tell that his joy was overflowing, even in a prison. And the Roman prisons were pretty tough.

FROST: Who do you think is the most important religious leader of the twentieth century?

GRAHAM: I would think that would be, possibly, Pope John. I think that he opened a gigantic Pandora's box within the Church of Rome that has affected the whole of the world church. I'm not a historian enough, or theologian enough to know exactly where it's going to take us or fully what's happening, but something of major proportions—a revolution within the church—is taking place. It's taking place within Protestantism; it's taking place within the Church of Rome; it's taking place in the Orthodox Church. I think that possibly I would put alongside that an American evangelist by the name of Dwight L. Moody—because from Moody came the British Labor Party . . .

FROST: I think the British public would be very mixed in their feelings about whether to commend him or not.

GRAHAM: Well, they would now, yes. That might . . .

FROST: Yes.

GRAHAM: But I mean there were many things that came from Moody politically, socially, and religiously, because he really was the founder of the modern ecumenical movement. The ecumenical movement was born in the great Northfield conferences that Moody conducted. Now Moody had very little education. He used the words "ain't" and "hain't" in the pulpit. The way the British Labor Party came about is interesting. He was preaching in Scotland and a young Scottish fellow was converted to Christ, and came to Mr. Moody and said, "I would like to work for God. What should I do?" Moody said, "Help the laboring people of Scotland." That fellow's name was Kerr Hardy. He became an evangelist and was an evangelist all of his life, but he was interested in bettering the working conditions of the people and his work led to the founding of the British Labor Party. Later the Fabians came in, but that evangelical wing has always been in the Labor Party.

FROST: You mentioned Pope John. A lot of people feel that the great problem facing the world is overpopulation. How do you feel about the current Pope's ban on the pill?

GRAHAM: Well, that . . .

FROST: Do you regret that?

GRAHAM: Yes, I do. I sympathize with the Pope because of the pressures that he felt within the Church and his own tradition and background. But I disagree. Because I don't think that there is anything in the Bible that teaches that sex

[78]

is just for the propagation of the race. Sex is to be enjoyed within marriage. It's to be the fulfillment of the marriage bond and not just to produce children. When one travels in India and the Orient and sees the pressure of population . . . In this country alone, in six generations, if the present population increase continues, do you know how many people there will be in the United States? Nine billion.

FROST: Nine billion . . .

GRAHAM: . . . Nine billion in America.

FROST: Potential television viewers.

GRAHAM: Or users of the product you're just selling. I don't know what you're selling. But we know that human nature cannot live that close together. This is going to bring about explosion. It's going to bring about famines. It's going to bring about war. It's going to bring about all kinds of problems, and we're rushing madly towards them now. We need some form of family planning and birth control. Somebody said that every third person born in the world is born by a Chinese woman. Somebody said, "Find that woman and stop her."

LAUGHTER

FROST: Looking at that, perhaps, as a mistake made by the Pope, would you, looking back at your life, pick on any mistakes that you made that, if you had the chance to live over again, you'd rewrite.

GRAHAM: Yes, if I had my life to live over again I would spend less time speaking and being interviewed and more time in study. I think that the pattern in the Scriptures is preparation for a rather short ministry. Christ prepared thirty years for three year's ministry. And I think that I have taken too many engagements and haven't spent enough time in the study, though I study an average of about six hours a day. But that's not enough, because the more I study, the more fields I find I want to study. Another mistake I think I have made is that when great spiritual movements got under way, under my leadership, after a period of time when I grew tired and weary of body, I left. I should have stayed. I should have stayed in Britain in 1954 because every city in Britain was asking us to come. The whole field was open. The press was with me, the television was with us. I think we could have capitalized on that in the provinces.

FROST: Yes. I don't quite know what the revival you talk about—moral, spiritual revival—exactly would mean, but I would have thought that Britain was on the verge of it then if you'd stayed. Certainly. How would you explain, not in huge theological terms, but in specifics, what it would be like if America had the moral and spiritual revival you preach about? How would that change all of our lives every day? I know it would mean the nation coming to God and all that, but how would it actually change this audience's lives?

GRAHAM: David, I think that it would produce a new atmosphere. I don't think it would solve traffic problems or the management-labor problems, or totally solve the race problem. But I think we would approach our problems in a new atmosphere in which we would think of the other person's point of view as much as we'd think of our own point of view. There would be a great deal more give and take, a great deal more consideration of each other's position. I think the wealthy people who live on Park Avenue would spend time up in the Bronx and in Harlem getting acquainted

*The evangelist meets Dick Williams (left) Oakland Athletics'
team manager, and Vida Blue (center), A's pitching sensation, in
the team's dressing room at the Oakland Coliseum.*

with the people there. I was with a man some time ago riding in his big Cadillac. As we drove through one of these areas of underprivileged people, I told him that I'd been in a home recently where nine people lived in one room. "Oh," he said, "Don't tell me that. I don't even want to think about it." Well this is something he ought to think about. This is something we all ought to think about. I think that if a person really knows Christ and is loving his neighbor as he should, he will not only think about it, but want to do something about it.

FROST: At the same time you don't really think that revival actually will come, do you, because you also believe in the Second Coming of Christ?

GRAHAM: I believe that it's possible that it will come because we have had periods of great revival in America as you have had in Britain. I think that a great case can be made for the fact that the great evangelical awakening of the eighteenth century saved Britain from the blood bath of the French Revolution. One could also say that a great deal of America's heritage comes from these great, sweeping revivals that have swept across the frontiers of American in the past. Whether we'll see it again . . . We may be seeing it now. It's not evidenced in church going, because there's a revolt in this country against the institutional church. It's also true in many parts of the world. But there's no revolt against believing in God, as the latest Gallup polls indicate. People are more interested in religion than ever before. I think that's evidenced in the tremendous crowds that come to these crusades and the tremendous amount of mail we get from our telecasts.

[82]

FROST: In that context, though, when do you believe that the Second Coming of Christ to this earth will be?

GRAHAM: I don't know. When the disciples asked Jesus that question, He said, "I don't know and it's not for you to know. Only My Father knows." Only God knows the answer to that. I personally think, the way the world is moving, that the signs that he left with us are converging at one point for the first time in history. I think that His coming may be relatively soon. Now by relatively, I'm not sure in your lifetime or mine, but certainly it's nearer now than when he made the prediction 2,000 years ago.

FROST: Safe. Very good point. Good prediction. What, before you go, what do you know of that will happen, what are you led to believe will happen when He comes again?

GRAHAM: Well, before he comes again the world is going to go through many convulsions, the Bible teaches. There will be worldwide lawlessness, there will be an overemphasis on sex, there will be an acceleration in technology. He said, "As it was in the days of Noah . . ." There will be a falling away from the Church. There are about twenty-seven signs that he left.

FROST: This makes it sound like tomorrow.

GRAHAM: That's the reason that I say "relatively soon" and I can go only so far as to repeat sooner than when He made the prediction.

FROST: But what will happen then. He will come . . .

GRAHAM: He will come and He is going to set up his kingdom. The ships will still sail the sea, the trains will still run, the planes will still be in the air and all the things that science is now getting a glimpse of will come true. Man will live for a

[83]

thousand years, death will be eliminated, the lion and the lamb will lie down together, the black children and the white children of Alabama will walk hand in hand. And it's going to be a marvelous world—the Utopia that people have dreamed of is going to come true. There will be social justice, racial justice, there'll be no war, there'll be no police forces—you won't need police forces—no crime. It's going to be a marvelous world, ruled by one man, Jesus Christ.

FROST: And the people will live for a thousand years. Right?

GRAHAM: Yes.

FROST: Well, now, what about all the people who are in heaven? Will they come back to earth, too?

GRAHAM: Yes.

FROST: Oh, so everybody will come back.

GRAHAM: Everybody will be here, and there will be far fewer than you think. Because He said that the gate to the road to heaven is very narrow. He made an interesting statement: He said, "Few there be that find it." And so we won't be over-populated at that time. It's going to be a marvelous world.

FROST: And when that happens, heaven will be here and there won't be anywhere else.

GRAHAM: I believe that heaven is still out in the future beyond that period. This period that I'm talking about, the Bible teaches, is going to last a thousand years, there's going to be another resurrection. There will be the resurrection of the godless—the wicked dead who rejected God. They're going to be brought to judgment and after that there'll be the new heavens and the new earth. The whole earth and the heavens will be renovated. The Bible tells about the New Jerusalem coming down. The twenty-first and twenty-second chapters of the Book of Revelation give vivid descriptions of what

[84]

heaven is going to be like. That's the permanent world, and that will be, I believe, the capital of the universe because I believe there is life on other planets.

FROST: The moon?

GRAHAM: Not the moon. I don't think the moon. But I think on other planets way out there in space, there's plenty of life. But have you ever thought about the fact that we might not recognize that life if we saw it. I mean, there may be other forms of creation that we possibly can not sense with our five senses. We've never developed electronics . . . I was told that by a great scientist—one of the greatest in the world—just the other day.

FROST: That we might not recognize life when we saw it?

GRAHAM: He went so far as to say that we're on the verge now of some sort of breakthrough of a new dimension in which this other world could have a train. This scientist, now this is not Billy Graham, this is not some wild thing I'm getting at, but they might have trains and run right through this room and you wouldn't even be conscious of it. Because it's another form of creation. This is a very interesting idea because the Bible speaks of "principalities and powers." We know there are demons and angels we can't see. We know that there are spiritual forces at work which we can't see. And without the microscope, you'd never have seen the germs. There's a form of creation that you'd never see without a modern instrument. And the same is true of the telescope. We're just on the verge of the most exciting things in the world. For example, if you were going to the nearest star, it would take an astronaut ten years to get there and back at the speed of light.

FROST: To the star?

GRAHAM: To the star—at the speed of light—186,000 miles a second. Now, when he'd get back to the airport here, he would only be ten days older because when you break the light barrier, and we might break the light barrier by 2000 AD, time ceases to exist. So that when the Bible teaches that God is "from everlasting to everlasting" and in the eternal present—everything is before and there is no past with God and no future—science now says this is absolutely accurate. There is no time when you break the light barrier.

FROST: That new world, I can see—the world of moon exploration—excites you. What about things like heart transplant surgery? Does that interest you or does it worry you . . . or what?

GRAHAM: Well, I got a letter the other day from one of the heart transplant patients in Stanford at Palo Alto, California, and I thought the letter would say "Mr. Graham, what about this new heart that I've gotten from another person? Does this change my relationship with God?" But he didn't at all. He told me that he had been converted in one of my crusades in 1950 and he was rejoicing in Christ and what God was doing for him, because the heart in the Bible is only a symbol of the inner man, of the spirit, of the soul. It is not a physical organ. I am all in favor of heart transplants under controlled conditions—in which death has actually occurred in the donor and in which there is little or no hope for the one who is going to receive it.

FROST: Well, that's what's terrifying, of course—the definition of death. Because death has changed.

GRAHAM: Right.

[86]

FROST: Because death has changed. You said we never discuss death. I discussed it, in fact, recently with Denton Cooley and I mean death has changed so much, hasn't it? I mean . . .

GRAHAM: As to what death is . . .

FROST: Is it a man's brain that decides that a man's dead? Or is it his heart? Or is it that his hair has stopped growing? You know what I mean . . . it's terribly . . .

GRAHAM: Right.

FROST: It's terribly difficult to know, you know, what death is. Does it worry you that we're reaching a stage where we've got too much control over our environment? I mean what about when we get to another stage where people will be able to genetically select what their children are like. That's a terrible responsibility.

GRAHAM: It is a big responsibility and these are areas, David, that I wouldn't dare comment on because I'll be very honest with you. I haven't thought them through and I'd rather not make a statement now that five years from now I'd have to say, "Oh, I regret that statement that I made to David Frost."

FROST: Well, you can come back here and say it.

GRAHAM: Well, thank you.

FROST: Thank you very much for being with us tonight. I enjoyed it so much. I hope to see you again soon.

GRAHAM: Thank you.

FROST: Thank you.

APPLAUSE

"The Bible says" is a phrase frequently used by Graham from the platform. He spends long hours studying the word of God in the privacy of his home study.

Billy Graham, the Dairyman's Boy

PROBABLY NO MAN IN HISTORY has preached to more people than Billy Graham. He is as well-known in Europe as the U.S., and there are few places on all five continents where his voice has not been heard.

Tall and striking in appearance with his blond hair and blue eyes, Billy Graham looks more like a movie star than a revivalist. Perhaps it is because of his appearance and his genial personality that he has made friends with the great ones of the world.

But none of this has caused him to forget his boyhood days on a farm on the outskirts of Charlotte, North Carolina. He was a normal boy who loved baseball and fun more than the religion of his devout parents. But at sixteen he was converted and the entire course of his life was changed. Upon graduation from Wheaton College in suburban Chicago, Graham was installed in a pastorate in nearby Western Springs. His contacts in the Christian world broadened when he was one of several men on the staff of the fledgling Youth for Christ organization.

But the "Christ for Greater Los Angeles" evangelistic campaign in 1949 shot him into national prominence. And soon the whole world was his parish. Through his television and radio programs, motion pictures, books, and his magazine, *Decision,* the ministry of Billy Graham has continued for a fruitful quarter of a century.

Billy Graham talks occasionally about concluding his evangelistic ministry, but there is every evidence he will continue to be heard for many years.

These interviews with David Frost display Graham as a loving husband and father. He comes across as compassionate and kind, and possessed of an uncomplicated sense of humor.

In short, on the David Frost Show, Billy Graham is not so much the popular evangelist as a charming Christian gentleman.

Mrs. Mona Frost, the performer's energetic mother, who lives in Beccles, a village southeast of London, was with her son when he entertained President and Mrs. Nixon at the White House.

David Frost, the Preacher's Kid

IN SOME OBSCURE COVE back in the southern mountains, there may be someone who has never heard of David Frost. A British television personality whom the polls reveal is known to ninety percent of the viewing audience in the United Kingdom, he has made it big on American TV too. He's the world's first commuting television performer, working two continents simultaneously.

Like his good friend, Billy Graham, David Frost was born into a devout Christian home. His father was a Methodist minister. David was only fifteen when he first heard Billy Graham conduct an evangelistic crusade in London's Harringay Arena. For a time at least, it looked as if he might be heading for the ministry. When he was nineteen, he was licensed as a local preacher. But show business had attracted him as early as age thirteen, when he staged a show in his father's church. At fifteen, he did parodies of popular television programs—still in the church. By the time he entered Cambridge, he had firmed up his desire to make show business his life work.

Frost today is completely absorbed in the entertainment

industry. He first came to the attention of American viewers as star and creator of a satirical television review of current events and personalities called, "That Was the Week That Was." Now he is known for "The David Frost Show" where he demonstrates his phenomenal ability as an in-depth interviewer of a range of celebrities.

In the first two years of its existence, the Frost Show has won an Emmy Award twice as the "Outstanding Musical or Variety Series." One of Frost's first guests when the program was launched in America was Billy Graham, with whom he spoke for ninety minutes—an unheard of record for television talk shows. Graham appeared eighteen months later for another ninety minute session, and these significant interviews became the inspiration for this little book.